# Crabapples

# Gymnastics

Bobbie Kalman & Tammy Everts
Photographs by Marc Crabtree

Crabtree Publishing Company

# Crabapples

## created by Bobbie Kalman

## For Allison Vernal with hugs and kisses

**Editor-in-Chief**
Bobbie Kalman

**Writing team**
Bobbie Kalman
Tammy Everts
Petrina Gentile

**Managing editor**
Lynda Hale

**Editors**
Petrina Gentile
Niki Walker

**Computer design**
Lynda Hale

**Consultants**
Brad May and Chris Foo,
Futures Gymnastics Center

**Special thanks to**
Brad May, David May, Chris Foo, Naomi Foo, Miguel Constante,
Jeff Soroksky, Lorraine Currie, Donna Nadanyi, Brent Cleal,
Nicholas Marotta, Brian Soares, Andrew Nadanyi, Maria Simone,
Lori Hamilton, Ivanka Koltalo, Tania Czobit, Jessica Anderson,
Fabienne Tougas, Terri Lynn Manna, Stephanie Muto, Ashley Tyrrell,
Brent Trull, Trevor Bain, Darren Trull, Christopher Lasachuk,
Kyle Olmsted, Pamela Peticovic, Alicia Harmon, Dylan Clapperton,
Ryan Peddle, Jessica Legault, Meghan Legault, and Wesley Paylor

**Photographs**
All photographs by Marc Crabtree

**Illustrations**
Rose Campbell

**Color separations and film**
Dot 'n Line Image Inc.

**Printer**
Worzalla Publishing Company

## Crabtree Publishing Company

350 Fifth Avenue
Suite 3308
New York
N.Y. 10118

360 York Road, RR 4,
Niagara-on-the-Lake,
Ontario, Canada
L0S 1J0

73 Lime Walk
Headington
Oxford OX3 7AD
United Kingdom

**Cataloging in Publication Data**
Kalman, Bobbie
   Gymnastics

(Crabapples)
Includes index.

ISBN 0-86505-631-5 (library bound)   ISBN 0-86505-731-1 (pbk.)
Gymnasts and gymnastic events, such as the pommel horse,
vault, high bar, and rings, are discussed in this book.

1. Gymnastics - Juvenile literature. 2. Gymnastics I. Everts,
Tammy, 1970-    II. Crabtree, Marc. III. Title. IV. Series:
Kalman, Bobbie. Crabapples.

GV461.K36  1996          j796.44          LC 96-42492
                                                      CIP

# What is in this book?

# Gymnastics

Have you ever watched a gymnast do backflips across a mat or twirl around a high bar? It takes hard work to be a good gymnast, but it is lots of fun!

stag elbow hold

There are eight different gymnastic events. Only girls perform on the balance beam and the uneven bars. Only boys perform on the parallel bars, pommel horse, rings, and high bar. Both boys and girls take part in floor and vault events.

back lever

For each event, gymnasts perform a number of moves, called a **routine**. Most routines begin with a **mount**, a move that gets the gymnast onto the equipment. The routine ends with a **dismount**, a move the gymnast makes to get off the equipment. Then the gymnast stands tall with his or her legs together and arms out straight.

# Warming up

Before doing any sport, it is important to **limber up**, or stretch. Stretching warms up the muscles. Warm muscles are not injured as easily as cold ones. The girls below are doing bridge exercises to stretch the muscles in their backs.

stretch

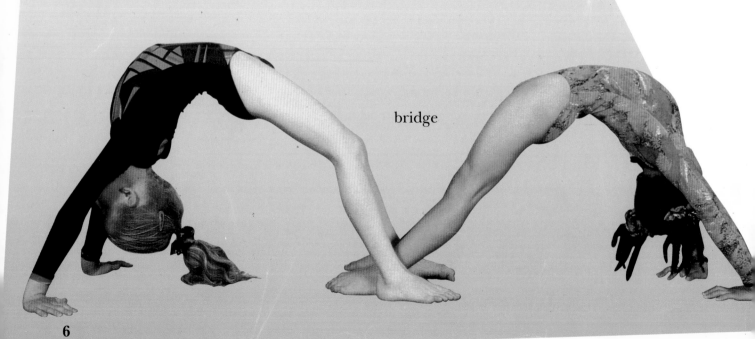

bridge

6

Stretching also makes muscles more flexible. Being flexible helps gymnasts move smoothly through a routine. It also allows them to bend their body into difficult positions. Stretching exercises, such as **over-splits**, are also used in routines.

over-splits

7

scale

# What you need

The most important thing a gymnast needs is a healthy body. Gymnasts also need special clothing. Close-fitting, stretchy clothes allow gymnasts to move freely. They also help a coach see if the gymnast is moving correctly. Boys wear a singlet and shorts. Girls wear a leotard.

handstand

Gymnasts practice and perform on special equipment. Rings, parallel bars, uneven bars, and the pommel horse are examples of gymnastic equipment. Some gymnasts wear **grips**, shown below left, for their routines on bars or rings. Chalk also prevents slipping and helps keep hands from blistering.

hip pull-over

# Safety

Some of the difficult moves gymnasts perform on equipment can be dangerous. Foam mats under the equipment protect gymnasts from hurting themselves if they fall. There are also other ways to stay safe.

Before trying a new move on the beam, gymnasts practice it on the floor until they are good at it. They work on the low beam until the coach says it is safe to move to the high beam.

A **spotter** stands by to make sure the gymnast does not fall. Adults make the best spotters because they are strong and able to hold young gymnasts. Spotters also help improve a gymnast's form and moves. They make sure that his or her body is straight.

bear walk

# Balance beam

front support

The balance beam is only ten centimeters (four inches) wide. Walking on it is very difficult for beginners! During a routine, it is important to keep moving and travel the entire length of the beam. Eyes should look straight ahead. No looking at your feet!

cartwheel

A beam routine includes a mount, some fast and slow moves, balancing skills, at least one difficult move, and a dismount. One simple move is the **pivot turn**. The gymnast stands on her toes and turns her body until she is facing the opposite direction. Other moves include cartwheels, rolls, handstands, and back tuck dismounts.

back tuck dismount

split leap

cast straddle off

# Uneven bars

The uneven bars is a beautiful but difficult event. Gymnasts must have good balance and strong hands and arms. They swing around the bars and move quickly from the high to the low.

Before a gymnast begins to practice on
the bars, she has to adjust them exactly
to her height. Each gymnast knows her
bar heights by heart. Gymnasts cover
their hands with chalk and wear grips
to keep their hands from blistering
when they rub against the wooden bars.

A routine on the uneven bars flows
smoothly from beginning to end. It
has fast and slow moves. A gymnast
might swing quickly around both bars
and then do a handstand on one bar.
She never holds one position for long.

swing

straddle inverted hang

swing

# Parallel bars

Parallel bars are the same height. Boys do not twirl around each bar as girls do on the uneven bars. A routine on the parallel bars includes swinging moves and **holds**. A hold is a position in which the gymnast stays for two or three seconds.

In competition, gymnasts also have to do at least one strength move, such as a handstand or straddle inverted hang. These difficult moves show both the balance and strength of the gymnasts.

mounting the bars

# Rings

The rings hang from the gym ceiling. They are high off the floor. A spotter must lift up the boy so that he can grab the rings. His routine will include swinging, hanging, and balancing moves.

muscle-up

back lever

It is important to keep the legs straight and together and the toes pointed. It is even more important to keep the rings from wobbling during the routine. Keeping the rings still is very difficult!

swing

# Pommel horse

A pommel horse looks like a padded box on two legs. It has two handles on top. The gymnast holds onto the handles as he swings around the horse.

During the routine, no part of the gymnast's body, except his hands, may touch the horse. Gymnasts must have strong arms and good balance to move smoothly through their routine!

support

flare

# Vault

The vaulting horse looks like a pommel
horse without handles. Gymnasts run
down a long mat to build up speed.
Then they jump onto a springboard
to leap over the horse. During this leap,
or **vault**, only their hands can touch the
horse. Their arms must stay straight.

Gymnasts do not just jump over the horse.
There are several different vaults, such
as the front handspring vault and the
squat-through vault.

"Here I go!"

front handspring vault

strength hold

front swing

# High bar

The high bar is also called the horizontal bar. High above the ground, boys swing, twist, and circle around a thin metal bar. They must have good balance and strong hands and arms.

During a routine, a gymnast has to change direction at least once. This move is very difficult. To turn around, the gymnast must hold the bar with only one hand. He has to make all the moves in his routine without stopping!

leg hip circle

# On the floor

The floor event is performed by both boys and girls. Boys tumble without music or dancing. Girls tumble and dance to music. Dancing helps connect their tumbling moves into a smooth routine. Some gymnasts study ballet to improve their floor routines.

left splits

scale

Floor exercises are done
on a large mat. Gymnasts
have to use the entire
area of the mat during
their routine.

pose

starting position for
a press to handstand

# In the air

aerial

Tumbling moves include forward and backward rolls, front and back walkovers, cartwheels, handsprings, handstands, and **aerials**. Aerials are somersaults and cartwheels that are done in mid-air. No part of the body can touch the ground.

back handspring

back tuck

Gymnasts practice tumbling moves such as back tucks and ring jumps. They perform several different moves during a routine.

ring jumps

# Eating right

A gymnast's body needs proper foods to make it strong and healthy. Fruits, vegetables, grains, meat, fish, and milk all make a body strong. A handful of raisins, a banana, a bagel, or some creamy yogurt are healthy snacks.

# Competitions

Gymnasts spend up to 20 hours a week practicing before a competition. You do not have to compete to enjoy gymnastics, but **gymnastics meets** are a fun way to make new friends, show off your skills, and maybe even win some medals or ribbons!

Gymnasts compete both in teams and by themselves. Each gymnast is awarded up to ten points for each event. In team competition, all the member's points are added together. The team with the most points is the **overall winner**. When gymnasts compete alone, the overall winner is the person with the most points. It does not matter who takes home a ribbon—everyone who tries hard is a winner!

# Young gymnasts

Every year, thousands of children study gymnastics. They work very hard. Many practice after school every day and on weekends! Meet some young gymnasts on these two pages.

Naomi loves doing splits, handstands, and cartwheels. She has won three medals and lots of ribbons!

Brent has been doing gymnastics for two years. His favorite event is the rings. When he is older, he also wants to learn the high bar.

Jessica started gymnastics when she was four. She practices 16 hours a week. Some days she starts as early as 8 a.m.!

Last year, David won his first bronze medal! His favorite event is the vault because he loves to do straddles and handsprings on it.

Maria has been a gymnast for four years and has won over 16 medals! The floor event is Maria's favorite because she loves to dance.

# Picture glossary & index

**balance beam**
pages 4, 11, 12-13

**high bar**
pages 4, 23, 30

**parallel bars**
pages 4, 9, 17

handles

**pommel horse**
pages 4, 9, 20

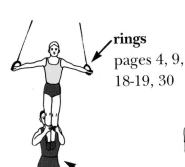

**rings**
pages 4, 9,
18-19, 30

**spotter**
pages 11, 18

**uneven bars**
pages 4, 9, 14-15, 17

spring-
board

horse

**vault**
pages 4, 21, 31

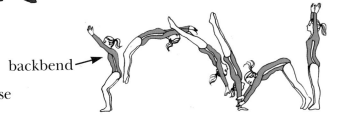

backbend

**floor routine**
pages 4, 24-25, 26-27, 31

1 2 3 4 5 6 7 8 9 0 Printed in USA 6 5 4 3 2 1 0 9 8 7